EAT
LIKE A
BEAR

Illustrated by
APRIL PULLEY SAYRE   STEVE JENKINS

HENRY HOLT AND COMPANY
New York

Can you eat like a bear?
Awake in April. Find food.
But where?

Drink like a bear—from a stream.
Leaping trout? None about.
Bushes? Bare. No berries there.
It's been four long months since fall,
when you were full.

Search the melting snows.

What barely shows?

Horsetails! Clip and snip. Eat sandy stems.

Dig in. Dig down.
Paw and claw and pull.
Find . . .

. . . a hide,
a starving bison that died in winter's cold.
Gnaw the frozen meat from its bones.

Can you search like a bear?

It's May. Find food.

But where?

Tear at sedges.
Chomp cow parsnip stems.
Eat dandelions.
Their yellow fluff
is not enough.
Sniff the air.
What smells?

A spruce, a slug, an early skunk.

Can you scratch like a bear? Find a tree.
Shuffle. Pause.
With long, strong claws,
dig in. Dig down.
Paw and claw and pull.
Find . . .

. . . ants!
Chew them,
sour and squirming.
Lick your lips.

Can you hunt like a bear?
It's June. Find food.
But where?

An elk calf has strayed from its herd.
Press paws. Give chase! Body bounding, race!
Find . . .

. . . you are left behind.

Hunting's over. Time for clover . . .
and for meeting another bear.

Can you bathe like a bear?
Ospreys and eagles
fight mid-air.
A cold stream awaits.
Wade in. Wade down.
Paw and claw and splash!
Find . . .

. . . a fish.

It thrashes. It bashes.

Swallow firm, fresh trout.

Can you forage like a bear?
It's July. Find food.
But where?

Search mountain meadows. Unearth roots.
Crisp, they crack.
A brown bear snack.

Wait. What was that?
Tilt your head.
Use your ears.
Dig in. Dig down.
Paw and claw and pull!
Find . . .

. . . a ground squirrel.
Grab and crunch
a meaty lunch.
Settle and snooze
as bumblebees buzz past.

Can you climb like a bear?
It's August. Find food.
But where?

Check the talus slopes.
Dig in. Dig down.
Paw and claw and flip!
Rocks
    tumble,
        crumble,
            crash and bounce!

Find . . .

. . . cutworm moths.
Mash them in your mouth.

Can you gather like a bear?
It's September. Find food.
But where?

Look for colors.
Is it time?
Are they ripe?
Scan up. Scan down.
Paw and claw and pull.
Find . . .

. . . huckleberries.
Rake them with
your teeth.
Purple your snout.

Can you eat like a bear?
It's October. Find food.
But where?

Follow tiny tracks.
Dig in. Dig down.
Paw and claw and pull.
Find . . .

. . . a squirrel's pinecone stash.
Nibble, shred, crunch, and smash.

Can you prepare like a bear?
Choose a site.
Here? Or there?
Gather branches and leaves.

Dig in, dig down.
Paw and claw and pull.
Hollow out a den—
the home you need.

Can you winter like a bear?
It's November.
The fat you wear
will help you live through winter.
Snows will come.

Settle in. Settle down.

Paw and cuddle and curl.

Find . . .

. . . midwinter, you have
two more mouths to feed.

MEET THE BEARS

BROWN BEARS

(scientific name *Ursus arctos*) live in North America, Europe, and Asia. The ones in the interior of Alaska and the lower 48 United States are often called grizzly bears. The word *grizzled* means "having gray-streaked hair." "Grizzly" refers to the silver-tipped appearance of grizzly bears' fur.

EVERY FOOD HAS ITS SEASON

Brown bears are omnivores, meaning that they eat many kinds of foods. What they eat depends on where they live and the season. The eating habits of the bears in this book were based on the bears of the Yellowstone National Park and Glacier National Park region. Elsewhere, brown bears wander ocean beaches and eat seaweed, crabs, and even the remains of beached whales. Bears will pluck plums, crunch into apples, and lick up honey. In coastal Alaska, Canada, and Russia, they wade into streams to eat spawning salmon that migrate upstream. According to the

U.S. Fish and Wildlife Service, Yellowstone's adult female grizzly bears weigh 200 to 428 pounds (91 to 194 kilograms), and adult males weigh 216 to 717 pounds (98 to 325 kilograms). Yet male brown bears of coastal Alaska, which feast on migrating salmon, can weigh as much as 1,400 pounds (635 kilograms)!

DO BEARS REALLY HIBERNATE?

Hibernation is when an animal's heart rate, breathing, temperature, and overall body functions decrease to save energy. Adult brown bears do not gather food, eat, or drink in winter. They stay in their dens. These dens are often tucked into north-facing slopes, where snow piles up and helps insulate the den entrance. Paws to nose, bears spend the winter curled up in a mostly quiet, sleepy state called "hibernation." Their bodies burn stored fat to help them survive.

For some years, however, scientists have debated over whether what bears do should really be called "hibernation." Although a bear's heart rate and breathing slow in winter, it does not become as cold or unresponsive as most other hibernators do. Loud noises may wake bears in winter. The females give birth to between two and four cubs in January or February, and they certainly wake up for that! During winter, the sleepy mothers also nurse their cubs. Some call bears "super hibernators" because adult bears, even the mothers, don't eat, drink, or pass

droppings during this time of winter rest. (Other hibernating animals must wake up now and again to do these things.) Despite bears' differences from other hibernators, most scientists now agree that bears do hibernate.

The newborn bear cubs do not hibernate. In their first months, they are awake, busy drinking their mother's milk and growing. The mother bear and her cubs stay in the den until spring. Each adult bear winters in its own den. The father bear sleeps in his own wintering den. The mother bear will raise the cubs on her own. They stay with her for several years.

WHAT TO EAT

When an adult bear emerges from hibernation, it can weigh almost a third less than it did when it went into its den in the fall. To restore its strength, it drinks from a stream or lake. It eats plants such as horsetails, which are green, gritty, and mostly stem. It searches for carrion—dead animals. (Elk and bison sometimes die from starvation or cold during the winter.) Brown bears also steal carcasses—already killed animals—from wolves. They might catch and eat young elk calves in spring, but by mid-June, many of the elk calves have grown big enough that their long legs allow them to escape.

The bears of the Yellowstone and Glacier National Park region can also take advantage of a yearly moth feast. Army cutworm caterpillars that have fed on weeds, alfalfa, wheat, barley, and oats in the Great Plains turn into winged adults and fly up into the Rocky Mountains. There they sip flower nectar at night. During the day, they rest in rocky areas, called talus slopes. A grizzly may dig out and eat 40,000 of these moths in a day.

GRIZZLIES: CHAMPION DIGGERS

Grizzly bears' long claws and strong shoulders help them dig into snow, soil, or rotten wood to find food. So throughout spring, summer, and fall, they dig for ants, termites, roots, and hidden caches— places where other animals have stored food. Red squirrels cut seed-filled cones from whitebark pine trees and store them in big piles under the ground or inside hollow trees. Bears search for these piles. Bears feed on pine nuts (pine seeds) not only in fall, but also in spring if seeds are left over from the previous year.

In years when pine trees produce a lot of nuts, bears are more likely to have cubs. (The pine nuts are nutritious and full of calories. They help the bears fatten up for winter. If a female bear does not put on enough winter fat, she is unlikely to produce cubs that year.) Whitebark pine trees are threatened by global climate change, which may be helping the spread of fungi and beetles that kill the trees.

BEAR FOOD, NOT PEOPLE FOOD

Handouts from people are not natural or healthy for bears. As recently as the 1960s, people visiting Yellowstone fed snacks to grizzly bears. Bears wandered along roadsides, begged for food, raided dumps, and damaged property. Dozens of people were injured each year during these interactions. Once bears know they can find food in backpacks, coolers, or trash cans, they begin to look for food in these places, which takes them away from their natural foods and puts them into situations where they conflict with humans. This makes people fearful, and bears may be shot or killed because of these encounters.

Beginning in 1970, Yellowstone park staff began to wean bears off people food. They banned bear feeding. They installed bear-proof trash cans. (Actually, saying the containers are "bear-proof" is a bit of a stretch. Park staff throughout the western United States must constantly work to improve their trash cans, because individual bears learn ways to get into the containers and the design has to be changed!) Bear poles, with ropes for hanging up food where bears have trouble reaching it, or bear-proof food storage containers are now provided at many campsites. Thanks to these efforts, most bears are ranging—and feeding—naturally throughout the Yellowstone region. Problem bears—those that do develop a taste for food from coolers and trash cans—are scared off by wildlife managers or relocated.

GRIZZLY BEAR FUTURE

Brown bears in the lower 48 United States are considered "threatened." Currently,

brown bears in Alaska are not listed as a threatened species.

SCIENTISTS WORKING TOGETHER TO STUDY BEARS

Brown bears, particularly those in Yellowstone, are well studied. Scientists from the National Park Service, U.S. Forest Service, U.S. Fish and Wildlife Service, U.S. Geological Survey, and other organizations gather their studies and exchange information through the Interagency Grizzly Bear Study Team (IGBST). Educators and young scientists wanting to dig into actual research papers about brown bears can find a list of dozens of studies done by members of the IGBST on the website of the U.S. Geological Survey's Northern Rocky Mountain Science Center at http://nrmsc.usgs.gov/science/igbst/detailedpubs.

AUTHOR'S NOTE

I awoke on April 10, 2008, thinking, *To be a bear*. To be a bear. What would it be like to be a bear? Over the next months, as the language for this piece unfolded, my work was bolstered by the many scientists and conservationists who first asked this question and walked in brown bear footsteps. My gratitude to them for publishing their findings and helping protect bears and their habitat. Folks who directly assisted me with answers, reviews, and references include Kerry Gunther of the Bear Management Office at Yellowstone National Park; Dr. Frank T. van Manen of the Interagency Grizzly Bear Study Team; Joseph K. Bump, PhD, professor of Forest Resources and Environmental Resources, Michigan Technological University; Carolyn Duckworth, then publications manager at Yellowstone National Park; and Horton Travis. My thanks to Noa Wheeler for terrific suggestions and to editor Laura Godwin, for her passionate work for bears worldwide.

For Gil and Laura —A. P. S.

For Robin —S. J.

Henry Holt and Company, LLC, *Publishers since 1866*
175 Fifth Avenue, New York, New York 10010
mackids.com

Henry Holt® is a registered trademark of Henry Holt and Company, LLC.
Text copyright © 2013 by April Pulley Sayre
Illustrations copyright © 2013 by Steve Jenkins
All rights reserved.

Library of Congress Cataloging-in-Publication Data
Sayre, April Pulley.
Eat like a bear / by April Pulley Sayre ; illustrated by Steve Jenkins. — First edition.
pages   cm
Summary: Follows a bear from the time she emerges from her den in April after four months without food, through months of eating fish, ants, and huckleberries, to midwinter when the arrival of two cubs interrupts her long winter's rest. Includes facts about brown (grizzly) bears of the Yellowstone National Park/Glacier National Park region.
ISBN 978-0-8050-9039-0 (hardback)
1. Grizzly bear—Juvenile fiction. [1. Grizzly bear—Fiction. 2. Bears—Fiction.] I. Jenkins, Steve, illustrator. II. Title.
PZ10.3.S277Eat 2013   [E]—dc23   2013015686

First Edition—2013 / Designed by April Ward
The artist used cut- and torn-paper collage to create the illustrations for this book. The bears are made with Amate, a handmade Mexican bark paper created from the bark of ficus (fig) trees.

Printed in China by South China Printing Co. Ltd., Dongguan City, Guangdong Province

1   3   5   7   9   10   8   6   4   2